The Rosen Publishing Group's
PowerKids Press™
New York

The VIKING LIBRARY

Viking Explorers and Settlers

Andrea Hopkins, Ph.D.

To my brother Matthew

Published in 2002 by The Rosen Publishing Group, Inc.
29 East 21st Street, New York, NY 10010

First Edition

Book Design and Layout: Michael Caroleo

Project Editor: Frances E. Ruffin

Photo Credits: Title page (Leif Erickson) © AKG Photo, London; title page (weather vane), contents page (top anchor), pp. 7 (Jelling stone featuring Christ), 12 (Brattahild) © Werner Forman/CORBIS; contents page (middle anchor) © Werner Forman Archive; contents page and p. 19 (arm rings) © The British Museum, London; p. 4 © National Geographic; p. 7 (Ikeq Fjord, Greenland) © Judith Lindbergh; p. 7 (Jelling Stone, bottom) © The Art Archive/Dagil Orti; p. 8 (ruins at Jarlshof) © Kevin Schafer/CORBIS; p. 8 (ship burning) © Ian A. Morrison; p. 11 (Ingolfur statue) © Nik Wheeler/CORBIS; p. 11 (Reykjavik) © Michael Nicholson/CORBIS; pp. 13, 20 (Norse landing) © Bettmann/CORBIS; p. 14 © Staffan Widstrand/CORBIS; p. 15 © Wolgang Kaehler/CORBIS; p. 16 (map) prepared by Marcia Bakry NMNH; p. 16 (Viking attack) © Hutton Getty/Archive Photos; p. 19 (spear and battle-ax) © Christer Ahlin, Museum of National Antiquities, Stockholm; p. 19 (Vikings sailing) © North Wind Pictures; p. 20 (Roman Forum ruins) © Ted Spiegel/CORBIS; p. 21 © Gianni Dagli Orti/CORBIS.

Images on contents page (arm rings) and pp. 8(ship burning), 16(map), 19(arm rings, spear and battle-ax) courtesy of the Artic Studies Center, Smithsonian National Museum of Natural History.

Hopkins, Andrea.
Viking explorers and settlers / Andrea Hopkins.
    p. cm. — (The Viking library)
Includes bibliographical references and index.
ISBN 0-8239-5816-7 (library binding)
1. Vikings—Juvenile literature. 2. Vikings—Europe, Northern—Juvenile literature. I. Title. II. Series.
DL65 .H67 2002
948'.004395—dc21

                                                                                    2001000254

Manufactured in the United States of Americas

Contents

1 The Viking Expansion   5

2 The Explorers   6

3 The Scottish Norse Kingdoms   9

4 The Icelanders   10

5 The Greenlanders   13

6 Greenland's Two Settlements   14

7 The Danelaw   17

8 The Irish Norse Kingdoms   18

9 Normandy   21

10 Russian City-States   22

Glossary   23

Index   24

Web Sites   24

GREENLAND

Svalbard

Spitsbergen

Baffin Island
(Helluland)

ca 1000

(Western
Settlement)

ca 985

Brattahlid
(Eastern
Settlement)

Reykjavík
Thingvellir
Vestmannaeyjar

ICELAND

ca 860

Faroe Is.

ca 800

Shetland Is.

ca 800

Orkney Is.

Lofoten

FINLAND

RUSSIA

*Aral
Sea*
(Chorezm)

Samarqand

Lake
Ladoga

St. Petersburg

Staraya Ladoga (Aldeigjuborg)

Bulgar

Velikiy Novgorod (Novgorod)

Volgograd

(Itil)

ASIA

*Caspian
Sea*

Gorgan

Trondheim

Uppsala

Sigtuna

SWEDEN

Sogne Fjord

NORWAY

Oslo

Bergen

Rebild

(Birka)

Stockholm

ESTONIA

LATVIA

Baltic

Visby

Gotland

Riga

Kiev

UKRAINE
(Berezany)

ca 1041

NORTH AMERICA

Labrador
(Markland)

L'Anse aux Meadows

(Vinland)

Newfoundland

New
York

*Cape
Cod*

Nova Scotia

Gulf
of
St. Lawrence

Atlantic
Ocean

Jutland

Århus

Skuldelev

DENMARK

Copenhagen

Roskilde

Jelling

(Hedeby)

Wolin

POLAND

EUROPE

Black Sea

North
Sea

SCOTLAND

Isle
of
Man

Holy I.
(Lindisfarne)

GERMANY

Prague

Dublin

York
(Jorvik)

Dorestad

IRELAND

WALES ENGLAND

Cork

Limerick

London

Quentovic

Rouen

Paris

Danube

ITALY

Rome

GREECE

Istanbul
(Constantinople)

TURKEY

Baghdad

Normandy

Nantes

FRANCE

Orléans

Bordeaux

Viking Routes

— Earliest
— Erik the Red
— Leif Eriksson
— Ingvar
-- Trading
⇒ Ocean current

Historical names in parentheses

0 mi   600
0 km   600

NG MAPS
ART BY LASZLO KUBINYI

SPAIN

*Strait of
Gibraltar*

Mediterranean Sea

AFRICA

ARABIA

The Viking Expansion

The Norse peoples lived in the cold countries of northern Europe–Sweden, Norway, and Denmark. From about A.D. 793, large numbers of Norsemen became Vikings. They left their homes to raid, rob, kidnap, and kill people in other European countries. Usually they went back to their homes afterward, but the Vikings were also hungry for land. As the numbers of people grew in their home countries, there wasn't enough land to go around. They wanted to find new places to settle in, or places where they could take land from the people who already lived there. In time Vikings started Norse colonies all over Europe. Their language, laws, and **customs** affected every **culture** they encountered.

◀ *The map shows the Viking exploration of Europe. The Vikings went to other European countries to raid them, but often they started colonies there and became part of the local culture.*

The Explorers

The Vikings were curious about new places and liked to explore. They sometimes told other people about their journeys. Often they carved messages on stones in **runes**, or they left other Viking objects behind them that showed where they had been. Some Vikings explored out of curiosity. Others looked for new lands to settle, or new goods to trade. They were used to living in countries with cold, harsh winters, where life wasn't easy. They didn't mind taking over other cold and harsh places, like Iceland and Greenland, where nobody lived. They also took over some places that were already **inhabited**, by force. The Norse started **colonies** in Europe's well-populated countries to the south.

Background Photo: *The Vikings were used to living in places that had cold, harsh winters, like at Ikeq Fjord, Greenland.* Inset: *Rune stones were decorated stones that marked Danish burial sites.*

The Scottish Norse Kingdoms

During the Viking Age, the Norse invaded several groups of islands off the coast of Scotland. These islands became Norse colonies and remained in Norse hands for many years afterward. The Isle of Man, midway between Ireland and England, was a great base for **raiding** on both countries. The people who lived there were **Celts**. The Norse began invading the island around A.D. 800. It remained a part of Norway until A.D. 1266, when the king of Norway sold it to the king of Scotland. The Orkney and Shetland Islands are two big groups of islands off the north coast of Scotland. Norse raiders **colonized** both island groups during the ninth century. They first belonged to Norway and then Denmark until A.D. 1472.

Background Photo: *Some former Norse colonies celebrate their Viking past. On the Orkney Islands, they hold a ship-burning festival, using reproductions of Viking longships.*
Top Left: *We learn about how Vikings lived from ruins such as those at Jarlshof on the Shetland Islands.*

9

The Icelanders

In about A.D. 870, Viking explorers discovered a large and almost empty island in the middle of the North Atlantic. They named it Iceland. According to Icelandic **sagas**, the first person to settle in Iceland was a Norwegian man named Ingolf Arnarson. He brought with him his family, followers, and slaves. He built a big farm not far from where Reykjavik, the capital city, is today. Thousands of people, mainly from Norway, followed Ingolf and settled in Iceland. Today Iceland has a population of about 274,000 people, many of whom are **descended** from those ninth-century Viking settlers. Their language is the closest of all the Scandinavian languages to the Old Norse spoken by Vikings.

Background Photo: *The city of Reykjavik is the modern capital of Iceland.*
Inset: *This is a statue of Ingolf Arnarson, the first person to settle in Iceland.*

Below: *The ruins of Brattahild, Erik the Red's farm, are still among the best land for farming in Greenland.*
Far Right: *This image shows Erik the Red fighting a man who was an Icelandic chieftain.*

The Greenlanders

In A.D. 982, a man named Erik the Red was **banished** from Iceland for killing some men. He sailed west to seek a new place to live. He found a new land that was empty and ready to settle. It was a huge island, almost covered with **glaciers**. Erik explored some parts of the coast, where there were many bays and creeks. The land there was green and good for farming. He chose a nice, sheltered place and built a farm. Erik wanted other people to come and live in his new land, which he called Greenland. In A.D. 985, he returned to Iceland and invited several hundred people to move with him. In the summer of that year, 25 ships set out from Iceland. Only 14 ships survived the heavy storms and arrived in Greenland.

Greenland's Two Settlements

The Greenlanders started a large settlement in the eastern part of the island and a small settlement in the west. To the north were hunting grounds where men could catch seals and walrus. There were plenty of fish and birds. They found valuable falcons, which could be used for hunting other birds and small animals. Even more valuable were polar bears. They were hunted and were given as gifts to kings and chieftains. Some Greenlanders, led by Erik's sons Leif and Thorvald, explored part of the coast of North America. They tried to start a settlement there but were driven away by Native Americans. The Greenland colony survived for more than 500 years before it disappeared without a trace.

Below: *The ruins of Greenland's Hvalsey Church still stand, although the last wedding ceremony took place in the year A.D. 1409.*
Far Left: *Greenland falcons, like the one shown in the inset, were valuable hunting birds for the Greenlanders.*

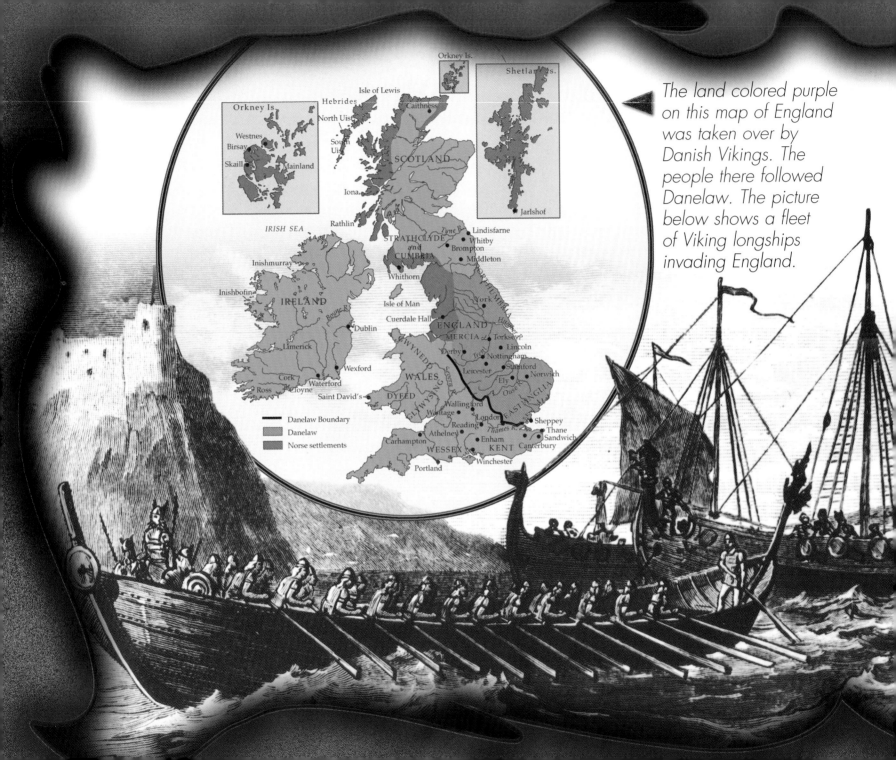

The land colored purple on this map of England was taken over by Danish Vikings. The people there followed Danelaw. The picture below shows a fleet of Viking longships invading England.

Orkney Is.

Shetland Is.

Orkney Is.

Isle of Lewis

Caithness

Hebrides

North Uist

Westness
Birsay

South Uist

Skaill

Mainland

SCOTLAND

Jarlshof

Iona

IRISH SEA

Rathlin

Tyne R.

Lindisfarne

STRATHCLYDE
and
CUMBRIA

Whitby

Brompton

Middleton

Inishmurray

Whithorn

Inishbofin

Isle of Man

NORTHUMBRIA

York

IRELAND

Boyne R.

Cuerdale Hall

Humber R.

ENGLAND

Dublin

MERCIA

Trent R.

Torksey

Derby

Lincoln

Limerick

Nottingham

Leicester

Stamford

Norwich

GWYNEDD

Ely

Ouse R.

WALES

Wexford

Cork

Waterford

DYFED

POWYS

EAST ANGLIA

Cloyne

Ross

Saint David's

Wallingford

London

Sheppey

Wantage

Thames R.

Thane

Reading

Sandwich

Athelney

Enham

Canterbury

Carhampton

WESSEX

KENT

Winchester

Portland

Danelaw Boundary

Danelaw

Norse settlements

The Danelaw

In A.D. 865, an army of Danish Vikings, led by Ivar the Boneless and his brothers Ubbe and Halfdan, came to England. A year later, they conquered most of the north of England. Nine years later, Alfred the Great managed to stop the Danes from taking over the whole of England. He made a **treaty** with the Danish leader Guthrum. They agreed that all land north of a line drawn east to west across the country would belong to the Danish and would follow Danish laws. Everything south of that line would remain under English control. Later this area of Danish rule was called the Danelaw. Thousands of Danes moved to England and started towns and villages with Norse names. Although Danish control of this territory didn't last more than 50 years, it forever changed the character, language, and customs of the people who lived in the north and east of England.

The Irish Norse Kingdoms

Ireland was one of the first places to suffer from Viking raids. In A.D. 840, a Norwegian Viking named Turgeis invaded Ireland with a fleet of ships and an army of men. First Turgeis and his men overran the towns in northern Ireland. Then they opened Norse-style, **fortified** trading centers in southern Ireland. Five years later, Turgeis was captured by the Irish king of Meath and was drowned in Lough (Lake) Owel. In about A.D. 850, a fleet of Danish Vikings invaded and captured the Norwegian **stronghold** of Dublin in southern Ireland. This was the first of many battles between the Danes and the Norwegians to control the **profitable** Irish kingdoms. To avoid being completely overtaken, the Irish kept the Norwegians fighting against the Danes.

Ireland was never completely conquered by the Norse, but Ireland never quite got rid of them, either. The small photos show Viking arm rings (top left) *and a Viking battle-ax,* (top right) *left behind in Ireland. The picture shows a fleet of Danish Viking ships.*

Near Right: *This painting shows Norse explorers landing on the coast of France during one of their many raids of European countries.*

Background Photo: *These ruins were once a large Roman marketplace that was raided by Vikings, who mistook it for the city of Rome.*

Far Right: *This is a nineteenth-century print of Viking leader Rollo, who became the Duke of Normandy.*

Normandy

In A.D. 885, a large army of Vikings attacked Paris and laid **siege** to it for a whole year. Finally the French king, Charles the Fat, came to Paris with his army. He couldn't defeat the Vikings so he paid them to leave. They wouldn't. France was a rich country and the Vikings wanted to stay. By A.D. 911, France agreed to let the Viking leader Rollo start a new state. It was called Normandy, the land of the North-men. Normandy went on to become very powerful. The Normans conquered England in A.D. 1066 and southern Italy and Sicily in stages from A.D. 999 to A.D. 1091. The Normans also settled in the Principality of Antioch, the Christian state in the Holy Land in A.D. 1098.

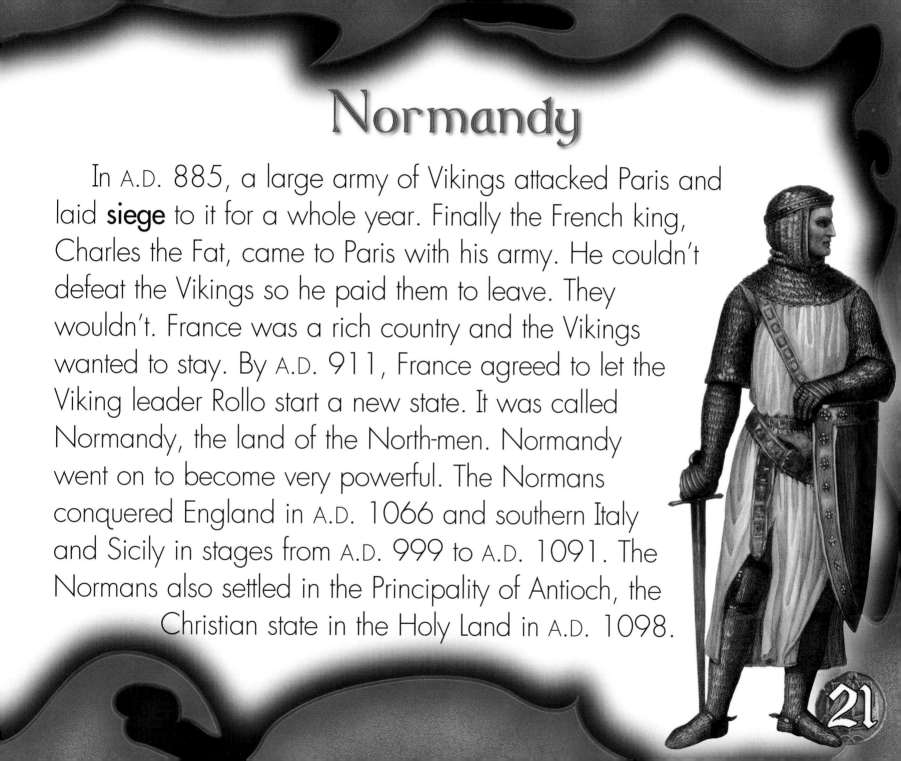

21

Russian City-States

There were Swedish Vikings who traveled to lands in eastern Europe to trade. The people in those countries called them the "Rus." Russia was named after them, though the Vikings called it "Sweden-the-Great" or "Gardariki" (fortress-land). They started trading centers protected by warriors. These centers grew to be large and successful cities. These fortified towns also allowed the Rus to control all of the countryside between the cities. For many years, the Rus ruled over the native **Slavic** people. The Swedish men ("Rus") had not brought Swedish women to their new colonies. They married Slavic women. In time the Rus became Christians, spoke a Slavic language instead of Norse, and forgot their old Norse customs and ways.

Glossary

banished (BA-nihshd) Having been forced to leave a country.

Celts (KELTS) A group of people from the British Isles and Ireland.

colonies (KAH-luh-neez) Areas in a new country settled by people who may still be ruled by the leaders and laws of their old country.

colonized (KAH-luh-nyzd) To have settled in a new land.

culture (KUL-cher) The beliefs, customs, art, and religions of a group of people.

customs (KUS-tumz) Accepted ways of doing something, often passed from parent to child.

descended (dih-SEN-did) Born of a certain family or group.

fortified (FOR-tih-fyd) Made stronger and more secure.

glaciers (GLAY-shurz) Large masses of ice that move.

inhabited (in-HA-bih-tid) Lived in.

profitable (PRAH-fih-tuh-buhl) Giving wealth or profit.

raiding (RAYD-ing) Attacking by surprise, usually by well-armed people.

runes (ROONZ) Alphabet used by the Norse people between the third and thirteenth centuries.

sagas (SAH-guz) Stories about the history and experiences of a people that are passed from one generation to another.

siege (SEEJ) When an enemy surrounds a city to force the people to surrender.

Slavic (SLAH-vik) Relating to the Slavs, people from Eastern Europe.

stronghold (STRAWNG-hold) A secure, well-guarded place.

treaty (TREE-tee) A formal agreement between nations or groups of people.

Index

A
Alfred the Great, 17
Arnarson, Ingolf, 10

C
Celts, 9
Charles the Fat (king of
    France), 21

D
Danelaw, 17
Denmark, 5, 9

E
Erik the Red, 13

G
glaciers, 13
Greenland, 6, 13, 14
Guthrum, 17

I
Iceland, 6, 10, 13
Ireland, 9, 18
Isle of Man, 9
Ivar the Boneless, 17

N
Normandy, 21
Norway, 5, 9, 10

R
Reykjavik, 10
Rollo (Viking leader), 21
runes, 6
Russia, 22

S
Scotland, 9
Shetland Islands, 9
Slavic people, 22
Sweden, 5

T
Turgeis, 18

Web Sites

To learn more about the Vikings, check out these Web sites:
http://home.ringnett.no/bjornstad/index.html
www.control.chalmers.se/vikings/viking.html